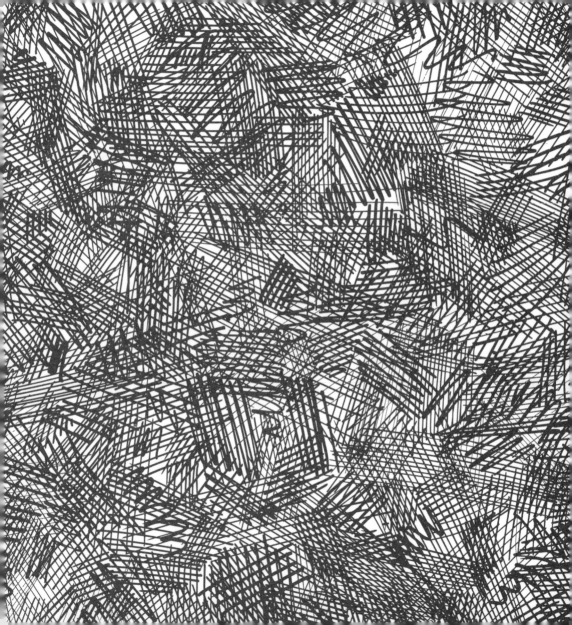

VOODOO ECONOMICS

If you can't even let me pay the check without feeling threatened,
how are you going to be able to start reporting to me?

VOODOO ECONOMICS

Cartoons by William Hamilton

CHRONICLE BOOKS

SAN FRANCISCO

To Gilliam

Printed in Mexico.

Library of Congress Cataloging-in-Publication Data

Hamilton, William, 1939-
    Voodoo Economics : cartoons / by William Hamilton.
   p. cm.
  ISBN 0-8118-0226-4
   1. Corporations—Caricatures and cartoons. 2. American
wit and humor, Pictoral. I. Title.
NC1429.H324A4 1992   92-1088
741.5'973—dc20   CIP

Book and cover design: Rob Hugel, XXX Design
Composition: Linotronic output by Hunza Graphics and Eurotype

Distributed in Canada by
Raincoast Books, 112 East Third Avenue,
Vancouver, B.C. V5T 1C8

10 9 8 7 6 5 4 3 2

Chronicle Books
275 Fifth Street
San Francisco, CA 94103

Operator, even though I find myself here in California, I don't think you should be calling me Eddie.

Merry Christmas, folks. And I want to say I wouldn't be president of this great company without the support of each and every one of you, or people very much like you.

Would it bother you to hear how little I paid for this flight?

*I'll have the businessman's lunch, Philippe, and bring my
son here the freelancer's lunch.*

Up front, Charlie. Have you ever negotiated with a woman?

At first, I admit, I really wanted power. But now, I don't know, maybe the trappings of power would be enough.

I used to love power, but now I'm more interested in mileage.

That's the kid I was telling you about—great natural hostility.

Sir, there are certain perks we consider inalienable perks.

*Marguerite? Hold on darling. I'm putting you in touch with Miss Witherspoon
who will handle my apology about last night.*

*Here she is Chief—and we'd be damn lucky to be getting her aboard
even if she weren't a woman.*

*Excuse me sir, but I forgot which parable we quote when
the stockholders start screaming.*

I can't stand this anymore. Why don't we watch some reruns of the eighties?

Oh, and your feelings have been trying to get in touch with you.

God, I was happy—crazy in love, and on a great per diem.

*Right on! I guess if I were still an executive vice president
I'd also have gone for the quail.*

*Look, Margo, I do not brag about how many hours a week I put in and
I haven't got time to argue about it because, as you know,
I put in a hundred hours a week here.*

Look. Let's just say I haven't seen anything, Charlie hasn't heard anything, and Tom hasn't said anything.

Call me old fashioned, but I like the way kids are thinking money again.

O.K. Let's say I'm one of these new mature spenders. Now: Appeal to me.

Professor? Remember how in "Lord Jim" a man wants to do good but instead he created complete disaster? And remember that stock I bought for you?

Yes, Phil, I'm afraid something is up. But, before we get to that, I just want you to know I never saw anybody who understood dressing for success like you; and that I'm going to miss your suits around here.

The image we're going to create for you is that of a man who doesn't give a hoot about his image.

It's all gone to hell. Sandy's been acquired, Herb disappeared
in a hostile takeover, Ted went into Chapter 11 to duck lawsuits, and now
Eddie's operation is changing its name.

Ethically speaking, there's nothing here that won't hose off.

I hope you boys don't mind Mr. Hayworth here sitting in. Mr. Hayworth is doing his thesis on yours truly.

You, sir, were my hero—until I became my own hero.

*Sirs, may I preface whatever it was you called me up here for
by saying how refreshing it is to get away from a lot of spoiled, overpaid kids
whining about rumors of a cutback?*

Nothing I say is written in stone unless I say it is.

Sure I like riding the booms—but what I love is defying the slumps.

If we're going to make it big and make it young, we better make it snappy.

31

Yes, Ted, on this team we take off our jackets, but we don't loosen our ties.

Research indicates our best shot is to come on as everybody's best-kept secret.

*How, specifically, did you break your company through the
traditional government safety nets?*

Not only have I been left on hold, it's been "Moon River" the whole damned time.

Oh, admit it, Tom—the only reason we merged was because everyone was merging.

*I want each of you to ask yourself if I have surrounded
myself with the best people.*

I got in on the ground floor—and I stayed there.

Greatness requires fame which requires publicity which is where we come in.

I think it's high time we quit shilly-shallying and put a couple of committees together to take a look at some of the contingencies of toughening our rhetoric!

*McLaughlin came over to us from them because he felt things could be done
better here, especially if we knew what was going on over there.*

*Let's face it. An agency paying top dollar for a copywriter
deserves the best. The very best. Me.*

I hear you're going for the big bad billion.

Rebecca? I got to thinking about my personal life and thought I'd give you a call.

I mean, you can have the cleanest air in the world but if you can't manufacture anything what the hell good is it?

Loved how you brought it all back to money.

Then, after lunch, there's the spontaneity workshop your new wife arranged.

We're not talking designer jeans here. We're talking designer genetics.

Martha and Lee are going to be doing our environmental hand-wringing.

Swallow us up and you'll have to swallow me up—and I'm a poison pill.

You need a little fresh air and publicity.

Shall we talk ninja to ninja?

Lloyd, I'll give it to you "al dente." You're fired.

I'll have the three martini lunch.

*I like to think that these old recipes you're learning at
Granny's knee may someday help you to work off executive stress from
your big, big business career.*

Scott, here, is my number two.

I see L.A. has given you permission not to wear a tie.

Mozart must have had days like this.

*Boys, boys. You're getting loud and no one here gives a damn
how big your salaries used to be.*

Damn, Langdon. That "Quién sabe?" of yours was about the suavest thing I ever heard at a board meeting.

We've checked, and it's fine with women.

It's such fun to hear stock tips again.

Only doubts about his masculinity kept him from openly crying.

We just come from completely different corporate cultures.

All you two have ever managed to show me is that no two flakes are alike!

If you have a baby, will you like it better than us?

You promised me the company on my sixtieth—and I don't think you're
being a very nice daddy and I hate you.

Say, where's that knowing little smile of the insider?

*Don't tell me they teach the gals how to brew coffee like this
at Harvard Business School.*

Don't cry. Mommy's going to be right back after she kills them in Detroit.

Mr. Lapham is going to be our sleaze factor.

I hear you bought yourself out.

You rose, Wally, but you never towered.

We need somebody smart to explain it to the prosecutor and somebody funny to explain it to the press.

O.K., Jimbo, let's dance with wolves.

Spike Kellogg World Headquarters. This is Spike.

And for God's sake stay as far away as you can from the legal system—
unless, of course, you're a lawyer.

Talent always fled the Midwest for New York, so it's only natural
that their state pension funds would follow.

Look, just forget what I said about quick fixes and easy solutions and come up with a quick fix or an easy solution.

Would you guys like to hear our new downturn specials?

Gentlemen, yours is going to be one of this period's seminal bankruptcies.

Well, enough from the brass section. Let's listen to the woodwinds.

Thanks again, Herb, but please try to remember, it's not me who's trying to woo you, it's my company.

*It's unanimous. Jan, you are now the first director of the
American Museum of the Leveraged Buyout.*

I'll tell you why we were put on this planet. We were put on this planet to outperform the market!

Am I a team player? Are you kidding? I was in a cult.

Look. Let's take a break and get these testosterone levels down.

*Now ask yourself—Did you really want this acquisition,
or are you just on the rebound?*

*And even up here at my level, I have to ask myself, do I really
need this many vice presidents?*

It's gone from two to four million six in five years. THAT'S
what I call art appreciation.

Who is our most creative accountant?

*We've shown them we can take the heat. Now let's show them
we can take the humidity, too.*

Last night, I got to thinking how mortified and embarrassed my
sweet and selfless mother would have been to discover her name on a big foundation.
So, this morning, I decided maybe we had better just go with my name.

*Mr. Arnold? The female stereotype we've been searching for
is sitting right in this office.*

All of a sudden, instead of architects and gardeners, your estate planners are lawyers and accountants.

Shall we go? I'm sure you don't want to watch me gloat any more than I want to watch you lick your wounds.

Why is it everybody on this team but me is always so angry and depressed?

California has always been too big for its britches.

Warn me if I'm talking above you. I'm on a very high concept diet.

*The turning point in my career, Dave, came when I was about your age and
the boss asked me to do something questionable. Now, Dave, would
you like to do something questionable?*

*Stan, we want you to go down to Brazil and make some
annoying generalizations.*

We're very excited about nuclear waste.

*Tom—I thought I'd better warn you: The chairman is
wearing the same suspenders.*

You'll be the centerpiece of the strategy—the bowl of fruit.

Put yourself in my position, Frank—wouldn't your first move be to weaken MY position?

Miss White, I thought I told you never to put through anyone who said they wanted to share something with me.

You can stop talking down. I'm an M.B.A.

They're here. Now remember, until I give the signal, we all play dead.

Leaving aside the legal absolutes, I think we have going for us some very attractive legal atmospherics.

Great! I put together a team and now I'm turned on by a gang.

You've made us terribly happy, and we hope you aren't feeling stupid.

I took because I had what it took to take.

The company's grateful "salute to you" dinner is in place and we're getting the spontaneous outpouring of affection on stream.

This won the Oscar for special effects in accounting.

He's so smooth I was halfway down on the elevator before I realized he'd fired me.

Now that your family company is part of our family of companies,
we've decided to put you up for adoption.

In a few years, we'll probably all be women.

Mom, it's Willy. I just fired off my first memo.

The tradition of sacrifice is as ancient as corporate culture.

Naturally, I don't know how you feel inside about this deal—but I know some self-congratulations are in order for me.

Skippy, when a person says she wants to have lunch sometime, it doesn't necessarily mean she ever really wants to.

*The new boardroom table, sir. Would you like to try
pounding on it before I sign?*

Many great men have known prison, but none of them, in all of history,
ever came away from it with as much money as will our speaker here today. . .

Who ever heard of a rock-solid liberal?

11 a.m., every day, I want a review of my wealth and fame, in that order.

*I'm insanely ambitious and I have this intense memory and
I'd never forget who first hired me.*

*We're talking an older, sixties type of guy, so don't be
afraid to talk about the Zen of it.*

S.P.—*I suppose you realize that around here you're becoming like a son to me.*

Loved your riff on morality.

Get your oars back in the cash flow.

It's the Feds. Why don't you take the fall—I mean the call?